Wonderful Words

A selection of short devotional articles

Compiled and Edited

By Michael Penny

ISBN: 978-1-78364-615-9

www.obt.org.uk

****

THE OPEN BIBLE TRUST
Fordland Mount, Upper Basildon,
Reading, RG8 8LU, UK

Wonderful Words

Contents

Introduction

These devotional articles first appeared on the pages of *Search* magazine over a number of years. It has been my pleasure to compile them, but they have required very little editing.

I am indebted to Karen Abbotts whose idea it was to pull them all together and publish them in a book, and who also typed them from the pages of the back issues of *search* and put them into one electronic file – which made my job so much easier.

The prayer of both Karen and myself is that readers will find this collection a helpful blessing.

Michael Penny

Accepted

Michael Penny

Last year I had a Christmas card from an old friend, and in it he gave me his email address. It was accepted@ ……. Many of my Christian friends use Christian terms as part of their email address, but I think this one is wonderful.

**All of us need to be accepted.
One, naturally, should be accepted by family,
and it is traumatic to a child when he is not accepted.
Friends are really those people who accept us.
We also want to be accepted at work
and in our community.
But the person we really need to accept us is God.
If He accepts us, we have eternal life.
If he does not accept us, we are doomed to perish.
(See John 3:16).**

So does God accept us? Yes! But how have we, sinners, become acceptable to the holy God? We read Ephesians 1:6 (*KJV*) that "he hath made us accepted in the beloved". We need to note two things here.

First, that it is God, not we ourselves, who has made us accepted; and second, we are accepted "in the beloved"; i.e. we are accepted in Christ. Christ is the only One who can make sinful humanity acceptable to God.

What does it mean "to be accepted"? The *ASV* puts it a little differently. It has "his grace, which he freely bestowed on us in the Beloved". Thus to be accepted, is to have His grace freely bestowed upon us. It is because Christ was the Lamb of God who took away the sin of the world that God can bestow His grace upon us and make us acceptable.

And the *NIV* has "his glorious grace, which he has freely given us in the One he loves". Here, to be accepted means to have God's glorious grace freely given to us.

But how do we obtain such grace? Simply by faith in Christ (Ephesians 2:8). Thus to be "accepted" by God, we must "accept" His Son as our Saviour. When He was on earth many did not accept Him. He said, "I tell you the truth no prophet is accepted in his hometown" (Luke 4:24). And sadly, today, many do not accept Jesus, but to all of us who do accept Him, He has ensured that we are accepted by God. What a privilege!

Approved

Mandrides Panos

**For he who serves Christ
in these things is
acceptable to God and
approved by men,
(Romans 14:18)**

We are Christ's ambassadors in the world. We form the church – the Body of Christ. Each member of that Body has some special talents and abilities.

Christ our Saviour, the Head of that Body, can use these talents and abilities to serve Him and spread the Word of God.

Our hands, feet, mind, tongue …. every single part of our body can be used effectively, with the help of the Holy Spirit, to do God's will exactly where it is needed the most.

So let us rise to the occasion and serve our Saviour with all our might.

The happiness we will have after serving Him faithfully will be beyond description, since we will feel the supreme feeling of all feelings …. God's approval.

**Be diligent to present yourself approved to
God a worker who does not need to
be ashamed, rightly dividing
the word of truth.
(2 Timothy 2:15)**

Bless

Michael Penny

The word *bless* is easily misunderstood. It conjures up in our minds a man decked in robes, making the sign of the cross, and pronouncing a formula which, supposedly, confers some supernatural favour or divine well-being upon the person or object being blessed! Yet this has little, if anything, to do with the wonderful biblical word *bless*.

I remember, many years ago, not long after becoming a believer, going with a friend to his church. There they *blessed* God. Having the above idea of bless, I wondered as to how we, poor, sinful, needy human beings, could pronounce any formula or say any words which would confer blessing upon God. And why did God need to be blessed anyway? Wasn't He the sum of all perfection? So what favour did He need conferred upon Him?

The Greek word for bless is *eulogeo,* which gives us the English words *eulogise,* meaning to extol, to praise, and *eulogy i*s a speech or writing commending or praising. This is precisely the meaning of *bless* and this word occurs three times in Ephesians 1:3. There we read, *"Praise* be to the God and Father of our Lord Jesus Christ, who has *blessed* us in the heavenly realms with every spiritual *blessing* in Christ."

This may be translated as follows: "Praise be to the God and Father of our Lord Jesus Christ, who has praised us in the heavenly realms with every spiritual praise in Christ." To me it is staggering that our God and Father praises us (i.e. blesses us). However, when I read that He praises us with every spiritual praise … then I am lost for words. How can this be? When each of us looks inside our own heart and acknowledges the type of person we are, how can the holy God of the Bible praise us with every spiritual praise? The answer lies in the last two words of the verse - "in Christ".

Of course, in myself there is little to praise. But when a person acknowledges that fact, and appreciates their need for forgiveness and a Saviour, and accepts Christ as Saviour, then that person is immediately placed "in Christ" and as such is "praised with every spiritual praise". And if we want just a glimpse of what this means, we need look no further than the next verse.

There we read that God chose us in Christ "to be holy and blameless in his sight". If that is the case, and it is, then no wonder Paul tells us to "Bless (i.e. praise, speak well of) the God and Father of our Lord Jesus Christ" for He speaks well of us….in Christ!

Blessed

Michael Penny

Some time ago we mentioned the word "bless" and how it means to "praise", to "speak well of", to "eulogise over" and is the Greek word *eulogia*. However, there is another Greek work which is also translated "bless" and that is *makarios*.

This is the word used in the *Beatitudes* in Matthew 5, where such people as the "poor in spirit" are said to be *blessed*, and the reason given is that "theirs is the kingdom of heaven". Similarly the "meek" are *blessed* because "they will inherit the earth". But what does this word *bless* mean? Basically it means to "be happy". Thus the Beatitudes could read;

- Happy are the poor in spirit, for theirs is the kingdom of heaven.
- Happy are those who mourn, for they will be comforted.
- Happy are the meek, for they will inherit the earth.
- Happy are those who hunger and thirst for righteousness, for they will be filled.
- Happy are the merciful, for they will be shown mercy.
- Happy are the pure in heart, for they will see God.
- Happy are the peacemakers, for they will be called sons of God.

Thus our Lord Jesus was telling the Jews of His day - who were the poor in spirit, the meek, the merciful, the peacemakers, the pure in heart and those who hungered and thirsted after righteousness - to be happy. Why? Because in the future, sometime in the future, when He comes and sets up His kingdom upon this earth, then they will inherit the earth and see God. Theirs will be the kingdom and they be called the sons of God. They will be comforted and shown mercy. If all that did not make them *happy*, then nothing would.

However, our Lord Jesus Christ also said something else about being *blessed* or *happy*. We read about it in Acts 20:35: "It is more *blessed* to give than to receive." In other words, we get more happiness by giving than we do from receiving! Is that true?

Our answer to that question depends upon our maturity. In the physical world this is easily seen to be true. Little children love receiving gifts and presents, yet never think of giving. They have to be taught to reciprocate by making little gifts for Nanny or buying a little present for granddad. And of course teenagers … well they are a law unto themselves! Quite often it isn't until we are parents ourselves that we begin to appreciate just how much happiness and satisfaction there is in giving and, of course, by the time we are grandparents it has become a great joy.

But what about us as Christians? Do we get great happiness out of giving? Out of giving to others; out of giving to church; out of giving to other Christian organizations like the Open Bible Trust? We should and giving can be a great source of happiness and contentment and that should not surprise us, even if it takes some of us a long time to learn.

But!

Michael Penny

How can the little word "but" be a *Wonderful Word?* As a conjunction "but" takes the meaning of yet, or nevertheless, or notwithstanding. As such it stands at the centre of two contrasting thoughts or statements. It is like the centre, or fulcrum, of old-fashioned weighing scales. Thus to some extent whether "but" is a *Wonderful Word* or not depends on the two things it is contrasting.

For me one of the most wonderful "buts" in Scripture comes in Ephesians 2:1-7.

> "As for you, you were dead in your transgressions and sins, in which you used to live when you followed the ways of this world and of the ruler of the kingdom of the air, the spirit who is now at work in those who are disobedient. All of us also lived among them at one time, gratifying the cravings of our sinful nature and following its desires and thoughts. Like the rest, we were by nature objects of wrath ..."

But

> "... because of his great love for us, God, who is rich in mercy, made us alive with Christ even when we were dead in transgressions - it is by grace you have been saved. And God raised us up with Christ and seated us with him in the heavenly realms in Christ Jesus, in order that in the coming ages he might show the incomparable riches of his grace, expressed in his kindness to us in Christ Jesus."

We were *dead* in our transgressions and sins ...
> **but** God made us *alive* with Christ.

We used to follow the ways of *this world* ...
> **but** God raised us up with *Christ*.

We used to follow the ways of the ruler of the *kingdom of the air* ...
> **but** God seated us with Christ in the *heavenly realms*.

We were objects of *wrath* ...
> **but** in the coming ages God is going to show us the *incomparable riches of His grace*.

Instead of being dead, we are alive. Instead of this world, we have Christ. Instead of following the ruler of the kingdom of the air, we follow Christ in the heavenly realms. And instead of objects of wrath, we shall see the incomparable riches of God's grace.

Yes ... "but" is indeed a *Wonderful Word* and there is another one in Ephesians 2:13. Please read Ephesians 2:11-18 and compare and contrast what comes on either side of that "but".

Choose

Michael Penny

One of the fundamental teachings of the Bible is that God has given his human creation choices. Adam and Eve had to choose between following God's way or not following it. And this theme runs throughout the Bible.

On leaving Egypt Moses presented the people of Israel with a wonderful proposition. If they obeyed God fully and kept His covenant, they would be His treasured possession, a holy nation and a kingdom of priests. In words they made the right choice, "We will do everything the Lord has said" (Exodus 19:3-8), but their actions soon showed that their hearts were not in that choice, and so roamed in the wilderness for forty years, so that they would know their hearts (Deuteronomy 8:2).

After entry into the Promised Land Joshua was still concerned as to whether this people would make the right choices. He called the leaders together and said:

"But if serving the Lord seems undesirable to you, then choose for yourselves this day whom you will serve, whether the gods your forefathers served beyond the River, or the gods of the Amorites, in whose land you are living. But as for me and my household, we will serve the Lord." (Joshua 24:15)

Those were the choices for Israel and the early Jewish Christians had similar choices. Peter put it quite clearly when speaking to them in Acts.

"It is by the name of Jesus Christ of Nazareth ... Salvation is found in no one else, for there is no other name under heaven given to men by which we must be saved." (Acts 4:10-11)

But if they chose Christ, that was not the end of the matter. Just like Joshua, Peter put before those early Christians choices they would face.

"We will continually face choices. For you have spent enough time in the past doing what pagans choose to do—living in debauchery, lust, drunkenness, orgies, carousing and detestable idolatry. They think it strange that you do not plunge with them into the same flood of dissipation, and they heap abuse on you." (1 Peter 4:3-4)

Today, we have similar choices, and it is up to us to make the right ones.

Compare

Michael Penny

It is easy for those who are well educated and who have some position in their church to put too much confidence "in the flesh", as Paul terms it. In other words, to feel that they have achieved religious acceptance by their education and position. Paul, certainly, could have boasted of his qualifications and status. For example, he could say that he was "circumcised on the eighth day, of the people of Israel, of the tribe of Benjamin, a Hebrew of Hebrews; in regard to the law, a Pharisee" (Philippians 3:5).

In the religious society of his day, this was an impressive history and even more impressive qualifications, but Paul had more; he had enthusiasm and dedication. His enthusiasm was demonstrated by him persecuting the church, and his dedication is summed up quite simply by "as for legalistic righteousness ... faultless" (3:6). What a statement: to be considered "faultless". What a man!

But ... and Paul follows this statement with a "but". He goes on to say that all these things, everything, he now considered as nothing ... as nothing? Surely these were something? No! They were nothing when *compared* to the "surpassing greatness of knowing Christ Jesus my Lord". He considered his history and achievements as "rubbish". Why?

First let us note that Paul is **not** saying that they are meaningless and are worthless *per se*. He is saying that *compared* to knowing Jesus Christ they are worth nothing, they may as well be rubbish. Why is this? It because when we know Jesus Christ and are "found in him", as Paul puts it, we are given something very special, something very precious, something we could never, ever obtain ourselves. We are given a gift, "the righteousness that comes from God" and this comes through faith in Jesus Christ. Our own qualifications, our own achievements, our own goodness, our own status, may be significant and important in the denomination in which we move. However, to us they should count as nothing *compared* to knowing Jesus Christ and to having the free gift of righteousness that God gives to all who confess they are sinners and accept Jesus Christ as their Saviour.

So what religious qualifications do we have? Were we christened or dedicated? Were we baptised or confirmed? Did we go to university or Bible College? Do we have a degree or a masters, even a doctorate? Are we upright and respected members of our church and community? If we have all, or some of these, let us thank and praise God for them, but let us realize that none of them will acquire the gift of God's righteousness. God gives that to the self-confessed sinner, not to the self-righteous Pharisee (Luke 18:10-14) as Paul learnt.

Compared

Michael Penny

It is surprising how much human beings learn by *comparison*. When we are children this is how we begin to appreciate big and small, fat and thin, short and tall, dark and light. But the learning process does not stop there. Quite often, as adults, one journey is compared to another, not only in its distance and time, but also in the interest of the route. We compare people, one with another, and sadly we can also compare ourselves with other people, or with what they have and their position in life. Usually it is with people who have more than us, and who are in a better position than we are, and that can lead to dissatisfaction.

The Apostle Paul was not averse to comparison. He wrote, describing his troubles as "light and momentary" (2 Corinthians 4:17). However, when we read of the catalogue of problems Paul had they are far from light and certainly not momentary. Two chapters later he lists some of his troubles, hardships and distresses. They included beatings, imprisonments, riots, sleepless nights and hunger (2 Corinthians 6:4-5). Was Paul a masochist? No! Paul was doing two things. Firstly he was making a *comparison*.

> "I consider that our present sufferings are not worth *comparing* with the glory that will be revealed in us." (Romans 8:18)

And secondly, he knew that God would reward him for what he had suffered in the cause of Christ.

"For our light and momentary troubles are achieving for us an eternal glory that far outweighs them all." (2 Corinthians 4:17)

Thus by *comparison*, and **only** by *comparison*, the troubles of this life can be termed "light" and "momentary". They are "momentary" when we *compare* them with the glory that awaits us not just for seventy years, but for "eternity". And they are "light" when we *compare* them with that glory which will far "outweigh" them. This is what helped Paul through all his troubles and this is what will help us, also, provided we also "fix our eyes not on what is seen, but on what is unseen" and we realize that what is seen is "temporary", but what is unseen is "eternal" (2 Corinthians 4:18).

What trials and tribulations await us in this life? I do not know, but I do know what awaits us in eternity. In the "coming ages", God is to show us "the incomparable riches" of His grace (Ephesians 2:7). What can be *compared* to that?

Contentment

Laura Kestly

As I was preparing for an annual art show this past summer/fall, in which the theme was based on the 3 *'Lost'* parables in Luke 15, I had the opportunity to study these stories in depth, particularly, the 'Lost Son', as that was the one I selected to base my painting on. However, this is not my painting. This is *The Return of the Prodigal* by Rembrandt.

> And Jesus said, "There was a man who had two sons. The younger son took his inheritance and went away to a far country where he wasted it all by living recklessly. A severe famine arose in the country and he began to be in need. He ended up working for a citizen of the country, feeding his pigs and longed for the leftover scraps. He came to himself and after thinking how well off his father's servants were, decided to repent to his father of what he had done and ask him if he could be treated as one of the servants, since he felt himself unworthy to be called a son any longer.

> His father saw him and felt compassion, and ran and embraced and kissed him. The son said to him, "Father, I have sinned against heaven and before you. I am no longer worthy to be called your son."

> But the father had a celebration in mind … His son was lost … And is found. (Condensed excerpt from Luke 15:11-32).

The story of the *Prodigal Son* is a fascinating tale of repentance and forgiveness. Some aspects of this story recently came to my mind again, mainly the idea of contentment. It's truly sad that in many areas and times in life, contentment is absent. This can be when we lose sight of the true value of things and people – finding contentment again only after they've been absent from our lives and returned.

The prodigal son surely had that realization when he "*came to himself*" (vs. 17) after grovelling around in pig slop, due to his discontentment and search for '*greener*' pastures afar. We all, at times, take for granted things like our good health, financial stability, friends and family, only to appreciate them more when they go missing from our lives.

> There is great gain in godliness with contentment, for we brought nothing into the world, and we cannot take anything out of the world. But if we have food and clothing, with these we will be content. But those who desire to be rich fall into temptation, into a snare, into many senseless and harmful desires that plunge people into ruin and destruction" (1 Timothy 6-9).

Isn't it interesting that the father, in the parable didn't waste any time with lectures when his son came home, and instead welcomed him with an open embrace, focusing on celebrating his return with joy?

> Blessed be the God and Father of our Lord Jesus Christ, who has blessed us, in Christ, with every spiritual blessing in the heavenly places…in Jesus Christ we have redemption through his blood, the forgiveness of our sins…an

inheritance…and when we believed in him, were sealed with the promised Holy Spirit… (Ephesians 1:3-14)

For this reason … we have much to be content with and much to be thankful for.

Things that Pass and Things that Last
Laura Kestly

It's hard for me,
with a human mind
to see this stark contrast –
between the things that pass away
and the things that last.

The Bible clearly tells me
that treasures on earth will rust.
It is the heavenly treasures
I should work toward and lay up.

My mind must be content
with the things I do not see
amidst all earthly treasures –
my gaze on eternity.

And so like Paul,
please help me Lord,
whatever my state may be,
to be content as all things pass
but my heavenly home with Thee.

Depend

Laura Kestly

Depend: to rely; to rest with confidence; to trust; to confide; to have full confidence.

As summer fades and autumn approaches, the words of Isaiah 40:7 come to mind:

> **"The grass withers, the flower fades:**
> **but the word of our**
> **God shall stand forever."**

About a year ago I had to buy my first pair of reading glasses. I find myself having to rely on them more each day. When I was younger, I always wanted glasses. I loved to read books and call me quirky, but I guess I just like the way glasses made people look. Ironically, now that I have them, I like the way they enable me to look at things.

I started thinking that our faith and relationship with God, through Christ, is a lot like that (or it should be anyway). We should find ourselves depending on Him (more and more as we get older) to help us see and look at people and things through the proper light and (eternal) perspective.

Through His Word/eyes, our lens will never be too near or far-sighted (as is often the case when we look just through our own eyes). "Be not wise in your own eyes," Proverbs 3:7, 21:2.

I am blessed to have a 91 year old friend who still drags me out for coffee. I've known him for almost 8 years now. His mind is amazingly sharp and active but he has trouble with his balance. He used to be able to get by with the use of a cane. Recently, after recovering from a broken hip, he's assisted by a walker.

> "Trust in the Lord with all your heart. Lean not on your own understanding. In all your ways acknowledge Him and He will direct your paths." (Proverbs 3:5-6)

The key, as it says in verse 6, is to acknowledge Him – which means to recognize. I recognize that I need my reading glasses to see more clearly. My friend acknowledges that he needs his walker for stability or he may fall. We need the Lord to be our spiritual (unseen) eyes for us. This autumn, as the leaves wither and fall to the ground, let it remind us to put our trust in and depend on a loving, almighty God that has graciously given us a hope – an eternal future, through His son, our Lord Jesus Christ. (Eph. 1:7-12; Titus 1:2; 1 Tim. 1:17). See rightly through *His* lens.

Poem

Laura Kestly

Glasses provide eyesight for me
on things, without them, I can't really see.
God's Word's the same
(spiritually so)
It directs me along
the path I must go
My body does age
and my teeth will decay
My brain gets forgetful,
what more can I say?
As wrinkles form
and my bones get too frail
I'll depend on God's Word
it will always prevail.

Epignosis

Michael Penny

E-pig-no-sis! What's that? It sounds like a cryptic coded message to a sister, telling her to avoid pork! But no, it is the Greek word *epignosis*. What's so wonderful about that?

Well, *gnosis* is the word for "knowledge" and is used in the New Testament, especially of spiritual knowledge or knowledge of God. It gives us the word *gnostic*, and the Gnostics were a first-century group of Christians who claimed that they were 'in the know'. Sadly their knowledge conflicted with what was taught in the Bible.

If we put an "a" in front of "gnostic" we get *agnostic*. In Greek "a" is the negative, or opposite, thus an *agnostic* is a person who does not know. Again, we use this especially with respect to knowledge of God and so an "agnostic" is someone who does not know whether or not God exists.

Similarly with *atheist*. A *theist* is someone who believes in God while an *atheist* is someone who does not believe in God. But what has all this to do with *epignosis*?

As said above, *gnosis* is "knowledge", but what is *epignosis*? There seem to be two shades of meaning to this word. One is that *epignosis* deals with a 'deeper' knowledge, a 'fuller' knowledge. The other suggests that *epignosis* is the *ac*knowledgement of the knowledge we have.

In Colossians 1:9-10, Paul wrote: "For this reason, since the day we heard about you, we have not stopped praying for you and asking God to fill you with the *knowledge* of his will through all spiritual wisdom and understanding. And we pray this in order that you may live a life worthy of the Lord and may please him in every way: bearing fruit in every good work, growing in the *knowledge* of God."

In both of these passages the word translated "knowledge" is *epignosis*. However, is Paul merely praying for the Colossians to be filled with "knowledge" and to grow in "knowledge"? It seems to me that what the Colossians needed, and what we as Christians need today, is to be filled with a *deeper* knowledge of God's will, and then to grow in a greater *ac*knowledgement; i.e., grow in acknowledging God's will in all aspects of our lives. *Epignosis* carries both of these thoughts. God does not expect us to acknowledge what we do not know. However, He does expect us to acknowledge what we do know.

Epignosis is, indeed, a wonderful word, and the prayer of Colossians 1:9-12 is a wonderful prayer. We could make it our daily prayer.

Faith

Michael Penny

Faith! Such a simple word and one everyone knows and understands ... or do we? Well it simply means to believe, to trust. We have to believe in the Lord Jesus Christ, to trust in His death on the cross as the sacrifice for our sins. If we do, then we are forgiven, saved, reconciled, and have eternal life.

But then James goes and messes everything up by saying that "faith by itself, if it is not accompanied by works is dead" (James 2:17). In fact he says something far worse! "What good is it, my brothers, if a man claims to have faith but has no deeds? Can such faith save him?" (James 2:14).

I wonder what Paul would have said about that? Well we know what he would have said. "For it is by grace you have been saved, through faith - and this not from yourselves, it is the gift of God - not by works, so that no-one can boast" (Ephesians 2:8-9). So it would seem that Paul and James were at logger-heads! Or were they? Perhaps we should read the next verse. Ephesians 2:10 says, "For we are God's workmanship, created in Christ Jesus to do good works, which God prepared in advance for us to do."

Thus there seems to be some relationship, an intimate relationship perhaps, between faith and works. It is almost as if you can't have one without the other. If you say you have the one (faith) but haven't the other (works) then you haven't got the one (faith). Am I confusing you? I hope not!

I was helped greatly by William Barclay's *New Testament Words*. He writes: "Faith: *pistis*. In the New Testament 'faith' is a word with more than one meaning. We may distinguish five main lines of thought."

However, the line of thought I found the most interesting was the first one. "The main meaning of faith, the characteristically Pauline meaning, is total commitment to Jesus Christ (Galatians 2:16; 3:26; 3:34). It is accepting Jesus Christ at his word, *both in his demands and in his promises*." Now there's faith for you!

All too often we can emphasise the need to exercise faith in Christ's sacrifice for our sins, and in His resurrection from the dead. But do we, at the same time, encourage people to exercise that same faith in, for example, Christ's moral teachings or in the Christian graces? There is a danger that we do not and so people may turn to Christ as their Saviour, but may not turn away from their past life, for they do not believe it wrong. And they may not embrace the new life, because they do not believe it right, being best for themselves and being the will of God (Colossians 1:9-12).

Remember, true faith is "accepting Jesus Christ at his word, both in his demands and in his promises". How we love those promises! But those demands ...?

Fruit

George Bloemers

During the summer-time, fruit and vegetables abound, or should! What's needed is:

Good soil	New nature; new creation
Good root system	Faith & hope in action
Water to survive and grow	The Bible, the Word of God
Attentive care	Spirit led
Fertilizing; vitamins	Renewing of the mind
Protection	The Armour of God
Pruning	Testing and trials
Tender loving care	Commitments

Fruit is an important issue in both the Old and New Testaments. It is mentioned 147 times in the Old and 79 times in the New. It is used literally and also symbolically. For example:

- Genesis 3:7: Our first parents partook and made coverings of fig leaves.

- Genesis 8:11: Noah was greatly encouraged by an olive branch.

- Luke 6:43-45: Fruit symbolised Israel's downfall.

- Matthew 7:16-20: Our Lord Jesus spoke of good and bad fruit.

Galatians 5:22: The fruit of the Spirit
which bring a harvest of:

Love, joy, peace, patience, kindness, goodness,

faithfulness, gentleness and self-control.

The question is: who will be the benefactor of such a harvest?

Good works

David Mwangi

Those who have trusted in God may be careful to devote themselves *to doing what is good*. These things are excellent and profitable for everyone (Titus 3:8)

Be ready to do every good work, wrote Paul in Titus 2:14-15, for these things are good and profitable unto men. Anyone who believes there is a contradiction between Paul's writing about grace and the statements in the book of James about works should study Paul's letter to Titus more carefully. For in that letter there is a beautiful harmony of 'grace' and 'good works.' The faithful saying of Titus 3:5-8 teaches us salvation comes about by grace, and not our own works. That settles the issue.

But once reborn, created anew, we are expected to be ready for 'every good work;' "be ready to do whatever is good" (Titus 3:1). We are a peculiar people created unto 'good works' (Ephesians 2:10), therefore we must be careful to maintain 'good works,' even be zealous to perform them. Titus 2:14 states that we should be "A people that are his very own, eager *to do what is good*." And Paul says more about 'doing good' in:

> **Titus 3:1-2:** Remind the people to be subject to rulers and authorities, to be obedient, to be ready *to do whatever is good*, to slander no one, to be peaceable and considerate, and to show true humility toward all men.

Titus 3:8: Those who have trusted in God may be careful to devote themselves *to doing what is good*. These things are excellent and profitable for everyone..

Titus 3:14: Our people must learn to devote themselves *to doing what is good*.

A minister must not only teach this but must constantly affirm this principle of good works in his own life, as Titus 2:7-8 states, "In everything set them an example by *doing what is good*. In your teaching show integrity, seriousness and soundness of speech that cannot be condemned, so that those who oppose you may be ashamed because they have nothing bad to say about you."

Have!

Michael Penny

How can *have* be a wonderful word? Well I suppose it depends on *what* you *have*. Victor Hugo, the Frenchman who wrote *Les Miserables*, said that "The supreme happiness of life is the conviction that we are loved." Thus, to *be* loved is the supreme happiness, but is to *be* loved the same as to *have* loved? The Bible makes it clear that to *have* love is the greatest of all. In 1 Corinthians 13:1-3 we read:

> If I speak in the tongues of men and of angels,
> *but have not love,*
> I am only a resounding gong or a clanging cymbal.
> If I have the gift of prophecy
> and can fathom all mysteries and all knowledge,
> and if I have a faith that can move mountains,
> *but have not love,*
> I am nothing.
> If I give all I possess to the poor
> and surrender my body to the flames,
> *but have not love,*
> I gain nothing.

It is easy to misunderstand this and think, like Victor Hugo, that what Paul is writing about is having someone love us. However, nothing could be further from Paul's mind. He is, in fact, talking about the exact opposite. He is talking about "the most excellent way". He is talking about *having* love for others; not others loving us.

As sinful human beings we may think that greater happiness is gained from receiving, rather than giving. However, Christ taught the opposite (Acts 20:35) and mature believers have learned, by experience, this to be the case.

Similarly, as fallen human beings, we may think greater happiness is gained by being loved, rather than by loving. Again, the Scriptures teach otherwise, and mature believers have learned this is so. Sadly, Victor Hugo did not. However, it seems that another novelist did. In Charles Dickens' *A Tale of Two Cities*, the hero switches places with the husband of the woman he loves to free the husband from the guillotine. Why? Because he *had* love for her and his greatest happiness was her well- being, loving her and making her happy, even at the expense of his own life.

However, let us be glad that Someone did *have* love for us, and still *has* love for us. The love He *had* led Him to switch places with us, to die in our place, to die for our sins.

As we know what it is to receive His love, and as we know what to *have* love means, let us *have* love one for another.

Head!

Michael Penny

What does this word conjure up in our minds? Certainly not the 'face', nor the 'brain', but we do give great importance to the *head*. We see it as that part of us that guides and controls our body, but in looking at the word in this way, we are in danger of reading a modern idea about the *head* back into the New Testament. For example, Morrish, in his *New and Concise Bible Dictionary*, says, "As head of the church Christ removes entirely every other controlling or guiding authority. As the head of a man guides and controls his body, so Christ has complete control over His church."

Now this may seem very reverent and Christ-exalting, until we stop to think. If, over the last two thousand years, Christ has controlled and guided His church, over which He has had complete control, then He hasn't been doing a very good job! And He is still not doing a very good job, when we consider the parlous state of the Christian church as it approaches the twenty-first century.

Not only that, there is a danger that we will read such a view of *head* into such passages as 1 Cor. 11:3; "I want you to realise that the head of every man is Christ and the head of the woman is man". So, just as Christ has complete control over His church, a man has complete control over his wife! And she has to submit to her husband in everything because he is the controlling *head*, (Eph. 5:22-24). However, it is doubtful if the people of the first century saw the *head* in this way. Rather it was looked upon as the 'source' of all nourishment for the body (see *The Epistles to the Colossians, to Philemon and to the Ephesians,* by F. F. Bruce). It was through the *head* that the body took in food, drink and air. It was through the *head* that the body could see, hear, speak, and smell. All the body's needs were supplied by the *head*, and this is the sense in which Christ is the *head* of the church (Philippians 4:19).

In Ephesians 5:25-27 we are told, "Christ loved the church and gave himself up for her to make her holy ... and to present her ... without stain or wrinkle or any other blemish". Here Christ is seen to supply all the needs of the church. This is reiterated in Ephesians 5:29; "no man ever hated his own body, but he feeds and cares for it, just as Christ does the church".

So, when we look at Christ as our *head*, we would do better to see Him as the supplier of all our needs, rather than the one who has complete control over us. The former is true. The latter may sound very pious, but, if we are honest, it is not true.

Hope

George Bloemers

My *hope* is built on nothing less
Than Jesus Christ's righteousness

The words from a favourite old hymn of many, I'm sure, and we use this word *hope* every day in our lives but do we, as believers in Christ Jesus, really know what is at stake?

We hear "I hope so!" or "I hope to!" "I hope to pass my exams this year!" Hope so! Hope to!

But on the spiritual side, *hope* looks forward; future. It means expectation, but it is intimately linked with faith, and could be summed up as, "Faith is being sure of what we hoped for" or "Faith is the title deeds for things hoped for" (Hebrews 11:1). *Hope* is looking for the outcome of sure faith.

Many years ago when living in Los Angeles, California, during the riot era my hope was really at its summit, looking forward to the day when I could own a farm in the country. Although my faith was tested time and time again, my hope never ceased and in the course of time I moved to Wisconsin and bought a small farm.

God, in His mercy, grace and purpose has a plan, an eternal place for man, and He has made provision for us to be seated with Christ in the heavenly places (Ephesians 2:6). That is our expectation, our future, our *hope*.

Some Scriptures on *hope*

- Ephesians 1:18: Paul's prayer is that we may know the *hope* to which God has called us.

- Ephesians 4:1: We all have one *hope.*

- Colossians 1:5: The *hope* that is stored up for us in heaven.

- Colossians 1:23: The *hope* held out in the gospel.

- Colossians 1:27: Christ in us, literally among us, the *hope* of glory.

- 1 Timothy 1:1: Christ Jesus our *hope.*

- 1 Timothy 4:10: We have put our *hope* in the living God.

- Titus 1:2: A faith and knowledge resting on the *hope* of eternal life which God, who does not lie, promised before the beginning of time.

- Titus 2:13: We wait for the blessed *hope* – the glorious appearing of our great God and Saviour, Jesus Christ.

- Titus 3:7: He saved us … So that having been justified by his grace, we might become heirs having the *hope* of eternal life.

Hope

Michael Penny

In every-day language the word *hope* has some uncertainty attached to it. "I hope I will be able to make it. I will let you know." "I hope to be there Saturday night, but it depends on ..." The person may sincerely want to do what is hoped for, and the likelihood of them doing it may be most likely, even probable, but there is always some doubt attached to them being able to do or to have, what they hope for.

According to dictionaries *hope* is an expectation and a desire combined together. *To hope* means to desire, not with certainty, but with a belief that it is possible to obtain what is hoped for. Again, we see some doubt is attached to a person being able to realise what is hoped for.

Is this how the word *hope* is used in the Bible? Is the Christian's *hope* unsure and uncertain? Is there some doubt attached to it? Is it only a possibility? Or, at best, a probable outcome? If it is, then we are in danger of being pitied more than all men (1 Corinthians 15:19).

However, the Christian's *hope*, although having to do with the unseen and the future, is a "favourable and **confident** expectation". It is a "happy anticipation of good" (Vine's *Expository Dictionary of New Testament Words*).

Whatever our hopes for this life may be, they are bound to be transient, temporal, and uncertain. As Christ, Himself, said, "Do not store up for yourselves treasures on earth, where moth and rust destroy, and where thieves break in and steal. But store up for yourselves treasures in heaven, where moth and rust do not destroy, and where thieves do not break in and steal. For where your treasure is, there your heart will be also" (Matthew 6:19-21).

If we are confident in our eternal *hope,* then we will set our "hearts on things above". We will set our "minds on things above, not on earthly things". And we will know that when Christ appears, then we "will appear with him in glory" (Colossians 3:1-4). That is our *hope.*

Also, Hebrews 11:1 says that "faith is being ***sure*** of what we *hope* for and ***certain*** of what we do not see". Thus, the Christian's *hope* is ***sure*** and ***certain***, and of this we can be ***confident***, because our *hope* is dependent upon Christ and His sacrifice for our sins. Therefore, never let us waver in our commitment to Christ and let us "say 'No' to ungodliness and worldly passions" and let us "live self-controlled, upright and godly lives in this present age, while we wait for the blessed *hope* - the glorious appearing of our great God and Saviour, Jesus Christ" (Titus 2:12-13).

Hidden

Vicky Wilkinson

The reason I have selected the word *hidden* as my wonderful word is because Colossians 3:3 tells me that because I have been raised up in Christ, my life is *hidden* with Christ in God. What a wonderful thought to know that because we have believed, our life is so secure that it is *hidden* in a secret place with Christ in God.

Other things that the Scripture refers to as being hidden are: -

- The wisdom of God – This wisdom is spiritual wisdom and is *hidden* and revealed only to those who receive the Spirit of God. (1 Corinthians 2:7-16)

- All the treasure of wisdom and knowledge – These are *hidden* in the Father and Christ and tied up in the mystery of God. (Colossians 2:2-3)

- The mystery *hidden* from ages and generations – now revealed to His saints, which is Christ in you, the hope of glory. (Colossians 1:26-27)

- The fellowship of the mystery – from the beginning of the ages *hidden* in God – concerning Christ and the Church in the heavenly places. (Ephesians 3:9-10, 5:32)

- *Hidden* Manna – given to the over-comer in Revelation 2:17, which is the true bread from heaven, the bread of life. (Compare John 6:31-35)

Consideration of the above reveals that some wonderful things have been *hidden* in God the Father and Christ. Not only is our eternal life *hidden*, so that it is secure for the future, the Psalms show that the Lord is the person we can flee to at any time and be *hidden* in the time of trouble or anguish. "In the time of trouble, He will *hide* me in His pavilion" (27:5 *NKJV*). *"Hide* me under the shadow of your wings" (17:8).

With this in view we can join the psalmist when he says of the Lord, "You are my *hiding* place" (Psalm 119:114).

Image

Michael Penny

How can the word "image" be a *Wonderful Word*? After all, the Bible says a lot about not worshipping images.

There are two words for "image". First there is *eikon* which gives us the word 'icon', and which can be used in a bad sense; i.e. we should not worship icons or idols or images. However, this word is used of our Lord Jesus Christ in 2 Corinthians 4:4.

"The god of this age has blinded the minds of unbelievers, so that they cannot see the light of the gospel of the glory of Christ, who is the *image* of God."

The Bible tells us that no man has seen God, and no man can see God (in all His glory) and live. Thus if mankind needs to see God, and we do, then we can look upon Christ, Who is His *image*. Colossians 1:15-20 also uses this word of our Lord Jesus. "He [Christ] is the *image* of the invisible God, the firstborn over all creation. For [because] by him all things were created: things in heaven and on earth, visible and invisible, whether thrones or powers or rulers or authorities; all things were created by him and for him. He is before all things, and in him all things hold together. And he is the head of the body, the church; he is the beginning and the firstborn from among the dead, so that in everything he might have the supremacy. For God was pleased to have all his fullness dwell in him."

In colloquial Greek *eikonion* was used of a portrait which a young soldier had painted of himself and which he was sending home to his parents: a photograph in uniform! In other words, *eikon* is an *exact representation.*

R.C. Trench says of *eikon* that it "always assumes a prototype which it not merely resembles, but from which it is drawn". Thus when we read that Jesus is the *eikon* of God, not only does that mean that He resembles God, but that he is inherently and essentially connected with God.

This is brought home even more forcefully in Hebrews 1:3: "The Son is the radiance of God's glory and the exact representation (express image, *KJV*) of his being." Here, however, the Greek is *charackter*, which was the impression a seal left in wax, an impression which was an exact replica of the seal. In other words, *charackter* stresses the perfect likeness of Jesus to God.

However, *eikon* is also used of Christians in Colossians 3:9-10 where we are told, "Do not lie to each other, since you have taken off your old self with its practices and have put on the new self, which is being renewed in knowledge in the *image* of its Creator."

Thus our "new self" is being renewed in the *image* of its Creator, but how good an "image" is our "new self" of our Creator? If each of us is honest, we would have to say it is a poor image and, as such, we can see why Paul did not use the word *charackter*!

Love

Michael Penny

There is no greater experience in this life than "love" and yet it is a word that has become corrupted and debased by a decadent society. Samuel Butler's words in *Way of All Flesh* have been changed by a selfish self-centred society from "It is better to have loved and lost, than never to have loved at all", to "It is better to have been loved, than never to have been loved at all". That self-sacrificing love portrayed in Dickens' *Tale of Two Cities* has disappeared and gone. It has been replaced by a selfish love that lasts only so long as it benefits the one who, supposedly, loves.

All this forces us back to the Bible for we need to be reminded and refreshed by the perfect, self- sacrificial love that we see there. Archbishop Trench said of this love (Greek *agape*) that it is a word "born within the bosom of revealed religion". In other words, this love is not "human" love, but God's love and so we should not be surprised to learn that this word, *agape*, hardly occurs at all in secular Greek. Rather it describes the love of God, who "loved the world" (John 3:16) and who cares for all His creatures. Whether they are saints or sinners, "He causes his sun to rise on the evil and the good and sends rain on the righteous and the unrighteous" (Matthew 5:45).

William Barclay defines *agape* as "unconquerable benevolence, undefeatable good-will; it is the spirit that will never seek anything but the other person's good, no matter what the other person does". And the Apostle Paul, described this love in 1 Corinthians 13:4-8.

"Love is patient,
        love is kind.
It does not envy,
        it does not boast,
                it is not proud.
It is not rude,
        it is not self-seeking,
it is not easily angered,
        it keeps no record of wrongs.
Love does not delight in evil
        but rejoices with the truth.
It always protects,
        always trusts,
always hopes,
        always perseveres.
Love never fails."

Now there is "love" for you! And when we appreciate just what true "love" is, we realise just how far short we come in our love for one another and in our love for God. However, we also realise just how much God loves us, for even though we sin and come short, His love keeps no record of wrongs. He not only forgives our sins, but He also forgets them.

More on Love

Michael Penny

At a wedding I was conducting there was a rather interesting a misreading of 1 Corinthians 13:7. It was rendered "love preserves", rather than "love perseveres".

Recently, at another wedding, instead of the popular 1 Corinthians 13:1-8 being read, it was announced that a friend of the bride was to read about love from the *American Indian Bible*. I had never heard of this book before and, in my ignorance, thought it to be a different translation of the Bible. This idea was rapidly put to rest when I heard:

> For love should be given to those who can recognise love, receive love, or return love. Love should never be wasted on non-lovers or the result is the same as reproof is to fools.

How glad I am that God's love *is* "wasted on non-lovers". We are told that "God so loved the world" (John 3:16), which includes those who can recognise love, receive love and return love, plus those who do not love. And for this we should be glad, because mankind is a race of non-lovers. As 1 John 4:19 puts it, "We love because he first loved us."

The above words from the *American Indian Bible* display their human origins, by placing limitations on love, as we would all like to do! How different are the words of *the* Bible, which contain the mind of God? There we read that "Greater love has no-one than this, that one lays down his life for his friend" (John 15:13). There we read that "very rarely will anyone die for a righteous man" and that "for a good man someone might dare to die" (Romans 5:7-8). Here we have the heights of human life; to die for a friend or for a righteous man, or for a good man.

However, God demonstrated His own love for us in that "While we were yet *sinners*, Christ died for us" (Romans 5:8). Yes! "Christ died for the *ungodly*" so much so that even "when we were God's *enemies*, we were reconciled to Him through the death of His son" (Romans 5:10).

Thus, God's love was not and is not limited to those who recognise love, receive love and return love. He loves the world, including the ungodly, the sinners, those who are His enemies, and even those who do not recognise His love, receive His love or return His love. It is a poor sort of love which loves only those who love us. As Luke 6:32 puts it, "If you love those who love you, what credit is that to you? Even 'sinners' love those who love them." Let us rise above being 'sinners' and love those who do not return our love.

New!

Gail Nicholas

Old Testament: *Chadash.* The Hebrew word has the primary meaning of 'fresh' or 'new.'

- **NEW SONG:** Psalm 40:3 – "He has put a *new song* in my mouth even praise unto our God."

- **NEW THING:** Isaiah 43:19 – "Behold, I will do a *new thing*; Now it shall spring forth; Shall ye not know it?"

- **NEW MERCIES:** Lamentations 3:22-23 – "It is of the Lord's *mercies* that we are not consumed, because His compassions fail not. They are *new* every morning, great is thy faithfulness."

New Testament: *Kainos.* The Greek word has the meaning of 'qualitatively new.'

- **NEW CREATION:** 2 Corinthians 5:17 – "Therefore if any man be in Christ, he is a *new creature*; old things are passed away; behold all things are become *new*."

- **NEW MAN:** Ephesians 2:15 – "For to make in Himself of twain, one *new man*; so making peace."

- **NEW NAME:** Revelation 2:17 – "…and in the stone, a *new name* written which no man knoweth save he that receiveth it."

- **ALL THINGS NEW:** Revelation 21:5 – "and He that sat upon the throne said, 'Behold I make *all things new*."

- **NEW HEAVENS AND NEW EARTH:** 2 Peter 3:13 – "Nevertheless we, according to his promise, look for a *new heavens* and a *new earth*, wherein dwelleth righteousness."

- **NEW MAN:** Ephesians 4:20-24 – "But ye have not so learned Christ; if so be that ye have heard him, and have been taught by him, as the truth is in Jesus; that ye put off concerning the former conversation the *old man*, which is corrupt according to the deceitful lusts; and be renewed in the spirit of your mind; and that ye put on the *new man*, which after God is created in righteousness and true holiness."

  Colossians 3:10: "…put on the *new man*, which is renewed in knowledge after the image of him that created him."

Peace

Michael Penny

The United Nations has a "peace keeping corps". A company of soldiers from different nations of the world which are placed on the border between two warring nations, or strategically inside a single country to "keep the peace" between two dissident factions.

However, we must not read this twentieth century idea of peace back into the Bible. Today peace is a somewhat negative word, a "no" word. That is, we say there is peace between two countries if there is no war between them. We say there is peace in democracy because there is no physical violence amongst opposing political parties. We say there is peace between employers and employees, management and union, because there are no strikes. We say that an estranged husband and wife are at peace with one another because they are no longer arguing and bickering. As long as people are not actually disputing with one other, we call it peace. In other words, the mere absence of trouble is, as far as we are concerned, peace! This is *not* what the Bible means by peace.

We are well aware that the standard Jewish greeting is "*Shalom!*", peace. In the New Testament this is the Greek *eirene*. To greet people with "*Shalom!*" does not simply wish them absence of trouble, or freedom from conflict. Rather it is to want for them everything that is to their good; to wish for them every blessing God can give. All Paul's letters begin with a prayer for peace -Rom. 1:7; 1 Cor. 1:3; 2 Cor. 1:2; Gal. 1:3; Phil. 1:2; Col. 1:2; 1Th. 1:1; 2Th. 1:2; 1 Tim. 1:2; 2 Tim. 1:2; Titus 1:4; Philemon 3; and, of course Ephesians 1:2.

And in Ephesians Paul follows it with one of the most outstanding verses in the Bible. The verse, above all other verses, which really explains what *peace* is. "Praise be to the God and Father of our Lord Jesus Christ, who has blessed us in the heavenly realms with every spiritual blessing in Christ" (Ephesians 1:3). If peace is to wish someone every blessing God can give, then we, already, have peace for we have "every spiritual blessing in Christ".

Peace does not mean an uneasy resignation, a negative intolerance, or an over-anxious long- suffering. Rather it means a relationship in which people find in friendship and fellowship the completing and satisfying of their lives through enhancing the good in the lives of others. Peace is a right relationship between two people - man and man; man and woman; man, and God - and we have "peace with God through our Lord Jesus Christ" (Romans 5:1). This does not mean that God "tolerates" us and we stand simply because he is "long-suffering". Rather it means that God "blesses us with every spiritual blessing". Now that is peace!

Peace

Avril Job

My *Wonderful Word* is *'peace'*. It has its origin in the Old Testament, but is very common in the New. I found General Hawthorne's comments in *The Oxford Companion to the Bible* very enlightening.

Old Testament

Shalom, the Hebrew word, has many usages. The root ideas are well-being, wholeness, soundness and completeness. It was used

- As a courteous greeting;
- to describe good relations between peoples and nations; and
- to describe quiet tranquillity and contentment.

New Testament

Eirene, the Greek word denotes the opposite of war and conflict, and later came to describe a harmonious state of man. The distinctive idea about *eirene* in the New Testament is mediation through Jesus Christ. He is described as the peace which ultimately unifies humanity, reconciling humanity with God through His death.

Peace has a theological dimension. God is described as 'peace', and He gives peace to His people. Peace, in its fullest sense cannot be had apart from God. That is my experience.

Do not be anxious about anything, but in everything, by prayer
and petition, with thanksgiving, present your requests to God.
And
the peace of God, which transcends all understanding,
will guard your hearts and your minds in Christ Jesus.
(Philippians 4:6-7)

Redeemed

Michael Penny

How wonderful it is to be 'redeemed', to have 'redemption', but fewer and fewer people today understand these *Wonderful Words*, especially younger people.

These words are hardly used in ordinary conversation today, although a few people encounter them, generally when someone 'redeems' their mortgage from the bank.

Usually a mortgage is taken out for twenty-five years. Regular payments are made each month and at the end of the twenty-five years the money borrowed, plus interest, has been repaid to the bank and the person then owns the property. However, a person may come into some money and wish to pay off their mortgage early, maybe after fifteen years. The amount of money still owing, plus some extra, is paid to the bank and the mortgage is 'redeemed'.

Another use of this word is coming back into fashion. This time it is not with banks, but with pawnbrokers. A valuable object can be taken to the pawnbroker who will lend the person some money maybe for a few days, a week, or a month. At the end of the agreed period the amount loaned, plus an agreed extra, is paid to the pawnbroker and the valuable object is 'redeemed'; i.e. returned to its rightful owner.

An old nursery rhyme deals with this …

Half a pound of tuppenny rice,
Half a pound of treacle.
That's the way the money goes,
Pop! goes the weasel.

The 'weasel' was the valuable object taken to the pawnbroker. Quite often people were very poor, and the children would be starving. Half a pound of rice would be boiled in water and treacle added to sweeten it, and this would feed the family, maybe for a day or two.

However, we have been redeemed, not from a bank or a pawnbroker, but from Satan, sin and death. We have been returned to our rightful owner, our heavenly Father. And the price He paid for us was certainly more valuable than we are. The price paid was the death of His only begotten Son, our Saviour, Jesus Christ.

> "For you know that it was not with perishable things such as silver or gold that you were redeemed from the empty way of life handed down to you from your forefathers, but with the precious blood of Christ, a lamb without blemish or defect." (1 Peter 1:18-19)

Rise Above

Karen Bismark

But those who trust in the Lord for help will find their strength renewed. They will rise on wings like eagles; they will run and not get weary; they will walk and not grow weak. (Isaiah 40:31)

I can relate to the last part of that verse. Every morning I walk with my two children to school, we take a picturesque walk through Forfar, the lovely little town that we live in. My son and I first leave my little girl at her school and then I walk with my son about three quarters of the way to his school. When we part I usually walk straight home.

Physical strength

The journey to the schools is downhill, so that means that the return journey is up hill, and a fairly steep hill at that. Sometimes on the way home I do a little shopping or run a few errands. This adds more distance to the journey. When I reach the unit of flats in which we live I have to scale three flights of steep stairs before I reach my doorway. By the time I close the door behind me I am very weary and tired from the long walk and the steps.

If I have had no time to eat before leaving, or even taken time to swallow a cup of coffee, I feel faint. This is my daily routine. It is a difficult one, but the longer I keep it up the stronger my body becomes and therefore I am physically more equipped to handle the fainting feeling. My body even gains extra strength to ward off any flu bugs or other ailments which can creep up on us.

Spiritual strength

It is the same with spiritual strength which needs to be exercised as well; the first line of the verse says, "But those who trust in the Lord for help will find their strength renewed." Here again there is a part for me to play. Strength does not just come upon us; ask any gym enthusiast. It takes regular training and determination to reach a required goal.

If I neglect to wait upon my Lord and serve Him faithfully by a daily reading of His Word and then putting into practice what He says I must do I cannot expect to be a strong Christian. He gives me guidelines in His Word to help me. It is like any manual but if I toss it aside, how do I grow spiritually? Where would my strength come from?

Those who wait upon the Lord shall have their strength renewed, and only then can we stand against the enemy's attacks. Our enemy, the devil, waits patiently for us to become weak, before he attacks.

They will rise on wings like eagles

Eagles spend much of the day soaring, especially where high hills and sheer cliffs provide strong thermals. Golden Eagles are typically seen soaring high above mountain peaks, alone or in pairs, looking for prey. With his super vision, the eagle scours the big picture below him, and when he spots his prey, he focuses on that one thing and forbids anything to distract him.

Have you ever seen an eagle unsure of himself? He takes off from his perch, or nest and doesn't look back, he is not afraid to fall because he is confident of his ability to rise again. When he leaves his perch he knows what his aim is. When he is at his highest, he is *free*, all trouble is below him. The only thing on his mind is achieving his goal. He does not worry about his food and where it will come from. It is out there.

This helps me understand Matthew 6:31-33, which talks about not worrying. Jesus is teaching us to set our eyes on the Kingdom of God and what He requires of us. Though we like the eagle can see the big picture because of our sight range, our eyes should really be focused on one thing, 'what God requires of me' this is what we must be striving to accomplish every day. And when we do this we experience that feeling, "They will rise on wings like eagles," for without worry, and with the proper focus, we are free to soar on wings like eagles.

When I do my best to obey the teachings Christ gave, I too can be more confident within myself knowing I will be able to defend myself when the enemy attacks. Also my problems become a tiny speck beneath me.

New every morning

When I wake every morning, I ask my Heavenly Father to take care of whatever I will face during the day, and then I must practice my faith by leaving the day in His hands. Soon I begin to realize that my mountains which were tormenting me, no longer seem so big.

Galatians 6:9 tells us not to become tired of doing good; "When you are in service to the Lord, do not give up and exclaim, I am tired, or I am to old, let someone else do the work." Our Father never gets tired of working for our good. He is also the one who rewards us.

When you are daily working for the Lord, it somehow does not seem as tiring as when you are doing work for personal or financial gain. In fact once you start experiencing all the blessings reaped from a busy Christian life, you will experience true joy and you will be glad that you made the effort. You will feel the benefit of "those who trust in the Lord for help" and who "soar on wings like eagles."

Saints!

Michael Penny

According to one of my contemporary dictionaries, a saint is an "outstandingly devout and virtuous person", but is this correct? Many people connect the word with extreme holiness and religious piety. It is a word associated with stained-glass windows depicting St. Peter or St. Paul or St. John or St. So, and So!

However, when we turn to the Bible we see that the word saint is not used in this way at all. For example, Paul addressed his letter to the Ephesians "to the saints in Ephesus". As we read through this letter we find these Ephesian saints were told that they must no longer live as the pagan Gentiles did (4:17). They were told to put off falsehood and speak the truth (4:25). They were told not to let the sun go down on their anger and to no longer steal (4:27-28).

And if that wasn't enough, they were told to "Get rid of all bitterness, rage and anger, brawling and slander, along with every form of malice" (4:31). I am sure that we normally associate all of these with saints!!!

And it is no different in Colossians, another letter addressed to saints. The Colossian Christians were told to put to death such things as "sexual immorality, impurity, lust, evil desires and greed" (3:5). They were also instructed to get rid of "anger, rage, malice, slander and filthy language", as well as lying (3:8-9). Do these identify a saintly person?

However, the word saints is a word which simply describes "God's people". It was used of Israel in the Old Testament, and of Jewish and Gentile Christians in the Acts period. And it is the word used for believers in Christ in this dispensation also.

The Greek word for "saint" is *hagios* and its basic meaning is "different" or "separate". The Temple was holy because it was different from other buildings. The Bible is holy because it is different from other books. Christians are holy because they are different from other people in that they have been separated to God. Now they have the task of separating themselves from the world.

Saints, then, are people who are different from the rest of the world and it may be better to translate *hagios* as "God's people". However, the difference is not a difference which results in extreme holiness, religious piety, outstanding virtue or moral perfection. The difference comes from us being "separated to God" by our faith in Christ. Once we have made that commitment to Christ, we then have the task of "separating ourselves from the world". That is a process, and that will take time. Holiness is a journey, not a reached destination. Being a saint, then, means being involved in an on-going process, rather than having reached a final state. And no matter how well or how badly we separate ourselves from the worldliness around us, we are still saints in God's eyes, even if we are not in the eyes of other Christians. What a blessing!

Saints

Michael Penny

We have all heard of biblical saints like Saint Peter and Saint Paul. And then there are all those worthies such as Saint Augustine, Saint Patrick and Saint Christopher, although there are some doubt as to whether Saint Christopher is a 'full' saint! And nowadays, in Catholic circles there is a movement to make a deceased Pope John Paul II a saint.

Catholic award this title 'saint' only to exceptional and outstanding Christians, like Saint Francis of Assisi, and in paintings they are shown with a halo, whereas 'ordinary' Christians are not so depicted.

However, in the Bible, the word 'saint' (Greek *hagios*) is used of each and every believer in the Lord Jesus Christ. The word *hagios* literally means 'holy ones' and every Christian is 'holy' because they are 'in Christ.' He has taken away their sin and now they are 'holy.'

That does not mean that they no longer sin, far from it. Paul addressed his letter to the Ephesians to 'the saints' (Ephesians 1:1). However, some in that church were far from perfect. There was lying and drunkenness, disputes and quarrels, stealing and some struggled with the rife sexual immorality of the society which surround them; e.g. see Ephesians 4:17-19, 25, 28, 29, 32, 5:18.

However, in spite of all this they were 'holy and blameless' in God's sight (Ephesians 1:3). There is that word 'holy' again; the same word which is translated 'saints' elsewhere. However, God wants us to be holy as He is holy, and to be like that we need to separate ourselves from the ways of the world.

which is renewed in knowledge after the image of him that created him."

L	E	A	D	**M**	T	I	N	D	A	L
D	I	N	A	**A**	R	E	B	R	X	E
A	V	E	S	T	E	R	N	A	A	N
D	I	R	E	H	B	A	Z	I	L	D
P	E	T	H	L	U	C	A	S	E	E
F	R	E	T	O	J	Y	M	A	P	R
R	A	E	W	S	E	H	O	U	O	U
C	N	M	O	L	P	T	E	L	L	I
I	R	T	H	O	H	H	N	I	D	S
S	A	B	N	E	L	E	N	C	E	B
G	A	B	R	I	E	L	A	T	N	E

Beginning with MARTIN and moving up and moving down, left or right, one letter at a time, can you trace the names of nineteen Saints.

Search

Michael Penny

Search is, indeed, a wonderful word. After all, it is the name of this magazine! It was named after the Jews in Berea who "*searched* the Scriptures daily" to see if what Paul said was correct (Acts 17:11, *KJV*). The *NIV* has "examined". Thus, we encourage all our readers to *search* and examine the Scriptures to see if what we write is correct ... but beware!

We may recall the woman who had ten silver coins but lost one. She *searched* carefully until she found it (Luke 15:8), and when she found it there was great joy. The point of this parable is that in the same way, there is great "rejoicing in the presence of the angels of God over one sinner who repents" (v. 10).

The disciples, when they were sent out by the Lord Jesus, were told to "*search* for some worthy person ... and stay at his house until you leave" (Matthew 10:11). Who would be a "worthy" person?

And then there is God Who "*searches* our hearts" (Rom. 8:27); the One "who *searches* hearts and minds" (Rev. 2:23). And what does He find? That depends on what we have put there, and that may depend on how well we have *searched* the Scriptures ... but beware!

Then there were the Old Testament prophets who spoke of the grace that was to come and who "*searched* intently and with the greatest care, trying to find out the time and circumstances to which the Spirit of Christ in them was pointing when he predicted the sufferings of Christ and the glories that would follow" (1 Peter 1:10-11). These also *searched* the Scriptures, but the focus of their *search* was the salvation, the grace, the sufferings and the glories of Christ.

These stand in contrast to the teachers of Christ's day, to whom our Lord said, "You diligently study (*search, KJV*) the Scriptures because you think that by them you possess eternal life. These are the Scriptures that testify about me, yet you refuse to come to me to have life" (John 5:39-40).

Let us realise that the prophets of old *searched* the Scriptures to have a better understanding of the salvation, the grace, the sufferings and the glories of Christ. Let us realise that during the Acts of the Apostles Paul tried to convince the Jews "about Jesus from of the Law of Moses and from the Prophets" (Acts 28:23) and that the Bereans of old *searched* the Scriptures to see if what Paul said about Jesus was so.

There is nothing special in *searching* the Scriptures. It all depends on what we *search* for, or perhaps for **Whom** we *search*.

Sealed

David Mwangi

In the symbolism of Scripture, the *seal* signifies a finished transaction. In Jeremiah 32:9-12 we read, "And I signed the deed and *sealed* it, and took witnesses, and weighed the money in balances. "Jeremiah's purchase of the field was a finished transaction.

Then again in John 19:30: "When Jesus, therefore, had received the vinegar, he said, 'It is finished!'" That was the shout of victory. The cost of our redemption had been paid. The ordeal was over. The transaction was finished.

Ephesians 1:13-14 says,

> And you also were included in Christ when you heard the word of truth, the gospel of your salvation. Having believed, you were marked in him with a seal, the promised Holy Spirit, who is a deposit guaranteeing our inheritance until the redemption of those who are God's possession – to the praise of his glory. For this reason, ever since I heard about your faith in the Lord Jesus and your love for all the saints,

Yes! The Holy Spirit, Himself, is the *seal*, and in Ephesians 4:30 we read we are "*sealed* until the day of redemption."

Indeed, *sealed* is a *Wonderful Word* and all who accept His free-will salvation are *sealed*, are owned. They belong to Jesus Christ the Lord. Our security is in Christ. It is being *sealed* with the Holy Spirit of promise. What a blessing!

Sincere

Laura Kestly

The word that I'd like to share with you is the word *sincere*. So much of our world today operates out of impure motives. They try to capture our minds and ears with appearances of reality, but end up emptying our pocketbooks and pulling us away from the only relationship that provides us with our only since source of truth.

According to the Dictionary

The word *sincere* as defined by *Noah Webster's 1828 American Dictionary of the English Language:*

Pure; unmixed; being in reality what it appears to be; not feigned; not simulated; not assumed or said for the sake of appearance; real; not hypocritical or pretended.

Sincerely: of pure motive; honesty; with real purity of heart; without simulation or disguises.

According to the Scriptures:

- Philippians 1:10: … that you may be **sincere** and without offense until the day of Christ; being filled with the fruits of righteousness, which are by Jesus Christ, to the glory and praise of God.

- Joshua 24:14: Fear the Lord, and serve him **in sincerity** and truth.

- 1 Peter 2:2: As new-born babes, desire **the sincere** (without guile) milk of the word.

- 1 Corinthians 5:8: …with the unleavened bread **of sincerity and truth**.

- 2 Corinthians 2:17: …For we are not as many, which corrupt the word of God: but as **of sincerity**, of God in the sight of God we speak in Christ.

- 2 Corinthians 8:8: Prove the **sincerity** (genuineness) of your love.

- Ephesians 6:24: Love our Lord Jesus Christ **in sincerity** (incorruptness).

- Titus 2:7: Showing incorruptness, gravity, **sincerity.**

May all of us, as believers, be encouraged daily to choose to walk genuinely in the Spirit, with our love toward the Lord Jesus Christ and to others as well.

Suffering

Gerson Auxtero

You may have wondered why God allows His children to suffer. It may be in the form of illness, job loss, bankruptcy, depression, divorce, terminal illness, even death. Or it may be persecution from extremists because of your witness of Jesus Christ. These things happen to most, if not all sooner or later, whether we like it or not. We ought to know why our Loving Father allows such things to happen in the life of His children.

The Apostle Paul says, "For it has been granted to you on behalf of Christ not only to believe on Him, but also to suffer for His name sake" (Philippians 1:29). But why? Suffering is God way of exposing or revealing the real essence of our hearts, to ourselves.

> Deuteronomy 8:2 says, "Remember how the Lord your God led you all the way in the desert these forty years, to humble you and to test you in order to see what was in your heart, whether or not you would keep his commands."
>
> Jeremiah clearly declared, "The heart is the most deceitful above all things" (Jeremiah 17:9).

God allows suffering to come into the lives of His children in order to burn off pride, selfishness, unbelief, bitterness, lust, greed and all the works of the flesh that hinders us from being an effective witness of God's grace in our community.

God's ultimate purpose in and through us is to visibly display the very attitude of Jesus Christ in our fragile and weak lives and this can be accomplished through God's chisel – suffering. One author correctly observes as to the purpose of suffering in our lives by stating, "God wants to prove your faith is genuine; and trials provide the most reliable proof." He further states, "In this way God brings triumph out of our trials. From the pit of despair, He lifts us to the pinnacle of faith. Hard times make strong saints. There is no other way."

If we turn to the pages of the Bible, especially in the writings of the Apostle Paul, we find several simple, yet profound, perspectives scattered through his epistles to help us deal with our sufferings in Christ, and many come unexpectedly in our lives. In the verses below we see indispensable insights from the hand of God which can actively work in the worst moments of our lives.

- Romans 8:18: Our present sufferings are not worth comparing with the glory that will be revealed in us.

- 2 Corinthians 1:5: The sufferings of Christ flow over into our lives; so also through Christ our comfort overflows.

- 2 Corinthians 1:6: Our sufferings produce patient endurance.

- 2 Corinthians 1:7: Our suffering in Christ gives us the best experience we can have to encourage and comfort others.

- Philippians 3:10: Sharing the fellowship of Christ's suffering is worthwhile, and is important to our spiritual maturity.

- Colossians 1:24: Paul's desire was to rejoice in every suffering in life.

- Hebrews 2:10: Our present salvation (e.g. sanctification) is perfected/matured through suffering.

Through

Michael Penny

How can a preposition be a wonderful word? Yet *through* is a wonderful word. It tells us "the means" by which an action is accomplished or "the means" by which we can access something. What is the means by which we can access God's grace? How is His forgiveness accomplished? Our answer to that may depend upon our church or our theological position.

In the Catholic tradition the "sacraments" are "the means" of grace, and there are seven of them; baptism, confirmation, the Mass, penance, extreme unction (anointing with oil), holy orders, and matrimony. Participation is these is needed for forgiveness.

In Protestantism the term "sacrament" is usually restricted to just baptism and holy communion (the Eucharist), but there appears to be come confusion as to what a "sacrament" does. Certainly many Protestants would be horrified to think that either baptism or communion were "the means" to grace, yet there are many more who feel that unless they are baptised they cannot be saved, and that unless they continue taking the Lord's Supper, they will not be forgiven.

It is the wonderful word *through* which clears up all such confusion. When we look at the word *through* in the Scriptures, we learn that there are not seven sacraments, or two, but only one, and that one is not included in the seven or the two listed above!

In Ephesians 2:8 we read, "For it is by grace you have been saved, *through* faith." Faith is the only sacrament, the only channel to forgiveness. Faith in the Lord Jesus Christ as our Saviour is the only way to access God's grace. He, alone, is the way, the truth and the life; the true and living way. As Romans 3:22 puts it, "This righteousness from God comes *through* faith in Jesus Christ to all who believe. There is no difference."

The word "through" occurs many, many times in Scripture and it would be an exhausting study to consider each one. However, the reader may care to look up the occurrences of *through* in Ephesians; see 1:5, 7; 2:8, 13, 16, 18; 3:6, 7, 10, 12, 16, 17; 4:3, 6; 5:26 in the *NIV*. When you do this, you will see just how wonderful a word *through* is.

However, the expression "through faith" occurs just thirteen times in the Bible; in Romans 3:22, 25; 5:1; Galatians 3:22, 26; Ephesians 2:8; 3:12, 17; Philippians 3:9; 2 Timothy 3:15; Hebrews 6:12; 11:33; 1 Peter 1:5. I would urge the reader to look up and meditate upon each one to discover not only how wonderful a word *through* is, but also to see how sure and certain, and wonderful, are God's atonement, righteousness, justification, salvation, sonship, and approachability.

Together

Vicki Wilkinson

Although we might often enjoy periods of time on our own, with just our own company, doing our own thing, even so, no one likes to be truly alone for long. If you are married, as I am, then you know that your husband or other family members will be returning home to be with you. Even if you live on your own, most of us have family or friends with whom we like to spend time or see regularly.

The word I have selected as a wonderful word is *together*. Ephesians 2:4-6 is the first scripture I would like to refer to which speaks about our togetherness with Christ.

> But God .... even when we were dead in trespasses (sins), made us alive *together* with Christ (by grace you have been saved), and raised us up *together*, and made us sit *together* in the heavenly places in Christ Jesus.

Even now, from a spiritual point of view, we are raised up and seated *together* in and with Christ. So even when we spend time by ourselves we are never alone if we are believers. Christ is always with us!

Our togetherness with Christ also includes our togetherness with all Christian believers. Ephesians 2:19-22 explains that all believers are built *together* as a building for the habitation of God. That is why we are encouraged:

- to be "knit *together* in love" (Colossians 2:2);

- to "be workers *together* with Him" (2 Corinthians 6:1);

- "to strive *together*" (Philippians 1:27), and

- not to forsake the assembling of ourselves *together* (Hebrews 10:25).

The promise for the future is that we should be:

- "glorified *together* (Romans 8:17), and

- live *together* with Him (1 Thessalonians 5:10).

This is when we will take our seat in the heavenly places in our new glorified spiritual body *together* with Christ.

Virtue

Gail Nicholas

My Wonderful Word is **virtue.**

Virtue as an acronym:

> **V**ery
> **I**ntense
> **R**eaching
> **T**oward
> **U**nfeigned
> **E**xcellence

Old Testament

Chayil, the Hebrew word, has many meanings. A few of the uses are strength valour, substance, power, and worthy. (E. W. Bullinger says "strong in all moral qualities.")

> Proverbs 31:10: "Who can find a **virtuous** woman? For her price is far above rubies."

New Testament

Arete, the Greek word, is translated "praise" or "virtue", and carries the meaning of good quality or excellence of any kind, pleasing to God, courage, and fortitude.

2 Peter 1:5: "And beside this, giving all diligence add to your faith **virtue**; and to **virtue** knowledge."

Before we became followers of Christ, through faith, we were very good at sin. Now that we have this precious faith, we are called to strive to be the very best we can for His sake. In other words, to add to our faith – **VIRTUE**. Not just a "desire", but a "determination" to be pleasing in His sight.

> **Bear with each other and forgive**
> **whatever grievances you may have against one another.**
> **Forgive as the Lord forgave you,**
> **and over all these *virtues* put on love,**
> **which binds them all together in perfect unity.**
>
> **(Colossians 3:13-14)**

With

George Bloemers

With speaks of unity, union, united, togetherness, sometimes, completeness. Husband, wife, family, etc.

With speaks of identification.
    "With Christ;" simply a lovely thought.

Here are just a few mentioned in the New Testament.

- We died *with* Christ: Romans 6:8.

- We were buried *with* Christ: Romans 6:4; Colossians 2:12.

- We were crucified *with* Christ: Galatians 2:10.

- We were raised *with* Christ: Colossians 3:1.

- We were united *with* Christ in resurrection: Romans 6:5.

- God has quickened us (made us alive) together *with* Christ:
  Ephesians 2:5; Colossians 2:13.

- We are seated in the heavenlies *with* Christ in glory: Colossians 3:3-4.

    Oh! What He has done for us and *with* us.
    And so we have peace *with* God: Romans 5:1.

Words! Words! Words!

Brian Sherring

The ability to communicate is not confined to the human race. Many animals are known to be able to 'speak' to their own species, even if incomprehensible to us. But only mankind will be held responsible before the Lord for their words. This is clear from the book of Job, when the Lord calls Job's three friends to account, saying, "I am angry with you….because you have *not spoken* of me what is right, as my servant Job has" (42:7). Job spoke "what is right", he was one of the three men (with Noah and Daniel) that Ezekiel used as an example of saving righteousness" (14:14, 20) and significantly only James, who has much to say about the tongue, refers to him by name in the New Testament (5:11).

The Tongue

James emphasises the importance of words; the "tongue" holds a key place in holy living. "We all stumble in many ways. If anyone is never at fault *in what he says*, he is a perfect man, able to keep his whole body in check" (3:2) Whether anyone, apart from the Lord Himself (1 Peter 2:22) ever achieves this perfection depends on our understanding of the word "perfect" (*teleios*). For us it can never been understood in the same light as when applied to our sinless Lord; for us it has to take a secondary meaning such as Paul's usage in Philippians 3:15, "All of us who are *mature* (*teleios*) should take such a view of things." To be 'word perfect' is a characteristic of a mature believer, something that *can* be attained.

Like so many things in this life, words can be used for good or evil. James gives an example of this, "With the tongue we praise our Lord and Father, and with it we curse men, who have been made in God's likeness" (3:9).

The old children's doggerel, "sticks and stones may break my bones but names will never hurt me" is not true; words can affect beliefs, convictions, self-esteem (via flattery or criticism), feelings, morale, produce good and bad reactions, in extreme cases even to death – "the tongue has the power of life and death" (Proverbs 18:21). Like the comparatively small rudder of a ship, the tongue can be used to cause great movement, for good or evil.

- Do not let any unwholesome talk come out of your mouths, but only what is helpful for building others up according to their needs, that it may benefit those who listen. (Ephesians 4:29).

We are what we say!

Words express what a person is: "Out of the overflow of the heart the mouth speaks. The good man brings good things out of the good stored in him, and the evil man brings evil things out of the evil stored in him" (Matthew 12:34, 35).

And what is "stored in us" has a lot to do with 'words', i.e. what we read and hear. There is a saying that, 'you are what you eat', and the Scriptures speak of 'eating' the Lord's words. Jeremiah referring to the Lord said, "When your words came, I ate them; they were my joy and my heart's delight" (15:16; see also Ezekiel 2:8; 3:3). We are conditioned by what we 'eat' (hear and read) and that can have an influence on what sort of person we are. Words are character building.

Truth and lies

The devil, in the guise of the serpent, spoke the first recorded lie in Scripture: "You will not surely die" (Genesis 3:4). In the natural order of events, nothing is more certain than dying.

Sadly, lying, with its ugly sisters deception and falsehood, is part of everyday life in society today. In many contexts it is not even looked upon as wrong.

There are, of course, degrees of lying; fibs, white lies, lies of expedience etc.. How the Lord will judge these I cannot say. I do know however, that "the wrath of God" will be directed against those who "supress the truth" in rejecting God (Romans 1:18, 19).

Of all the words that we use, I believe that in the Lord's judgment, 'the truth' and 'the lie' are of first importance. John has much to say on this subject. To him, Christ *is* the personification of truth (1:14; 14:6 etc.) and the devil is the "father" (originator) of the lie (8:44).

It is as though they are two systems at enmity with each other. And as he says in his first epistle, "no lie comes from the truth." John is writing in the context of what people think and say of Christ: "Who is a liar? It is the man who denies that Jesus is the Christ" (1 John 2:21, 22).

In the final analysis the truth revolves around what Christ is to us. Just as lies are the devil's "native language" (John 8:44 *NIV*) so the truth emanates from the one who **is** the truth, and it is by "speaking truth in love" (lit.) that "we will in all things grow up into him" (Ephesians 4:15).

In our natural desire for life we eat and drink,
we talk and listen;
and in the same way with an insatiable thirst
we should devote ourselves to reading the words of God.
Nilus of Ancrya
(Greek monk and writer; c 430 AD)

About the editor

Michael Penny was born in Ebbw Vale, Gwent, Wales in 1943. He read Mathematics at the University of Reading before teaching for twelve years and becoming the Director of Mathematics and Business Studies at Queen Mary's College Basingstoke in Hampshire, England. In 1978 he entered Christian publishing, and in 1984 became the administrator of the Open Bible Trust, a position he held for seven years, before moving to the USA and becoming pastor of Grace Church in New Berlin, Wisconsin. He returned to Britain in 1999 and taught Maths at a Special School until 2004.

At present he is the editor and administrator of the Open Bible Trust. He has been chair of Churches Together in Reading for ten years, Chair of Churches Together in Berkshire for one year, and has been on the Advisory Committee to Reading University Christian Union for eight. He is lead chaplain at Reading College and is Head Chaplain for Activate Learning Colleges including the City of Oxford College, Banbury College, Blackbird Leys College and Bracknell and Wokingham College. He has appeared on Premier Radio and BBC Radio Berks on many occasions. He has an itinerant ministry which takes him into churches of different denominations, mainly in Berkshire and South Oxfordshire.

In 2019 the Bishop of Reading nominated him to receive the Maundy Money from the Queen for his services to Christianity, the Church and the Community and he was one of the 93 men selected by Buckingham Palace from across the United Kingdom, along with 93 women.

Some of the major works written by Michael Penny, published by
The Open Bible Trust include:

40 Problem Passages
Approaching the Bible
The Bible! Myth or Message?
Galatians: Interpretation and Application
Joel's Prophecy: Past and Future
The Miracles of the Apostles
Paul: A Missionary of Genius
James: His life and letter
Peter: His life and letters
Comments and Queries about Christianity
Comments and Queries about the New Testament
Introducing God's Plan (with Sylvia Penny)
Introducing God's Word (with Carol Brown and Lynn Mrotek)
Following Philippians (with W M Henry)
The Will of God: Past and Present (with W M Henry)
Abraham and his seed (with Sylvia Penny and W M Henry)

He has also written a number of study guides including:
Moving through Mark
Learning from Luke
The Manual on the Gospel of John
Going through Galatians
Exploring Ephesians
A Study Guide to Psalm 119
The Balanced Christian Life (Ephesians)
Search the Acts of the Apostles (with Neville Stephens)

For a full list, and for details of the above, please visit

www.obt.org.uk

Also by Michael Penny

Four good books on four great people

From the pen of Michael Penny

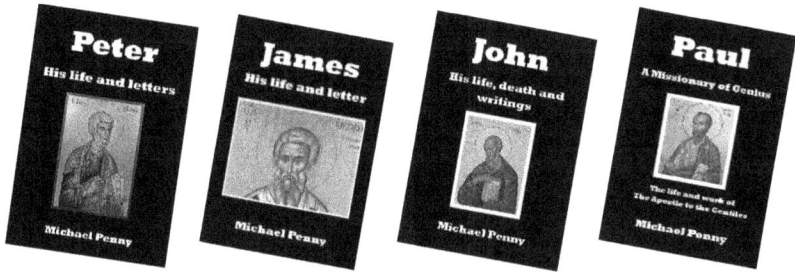

Peter: His life and letters

Peter! A solid rock or a moveable stone?

When did Peter first appear on the scene? What was he like as a person? What were his strengths and weaknesses? And what were the highs and lows of his life?

He denied Christ but became the immoveable force in the years following Christ's death, resurrection and ascension, but what happened to him after that?

This is a comprehensive and sympathetic treatment of one of the most important men in the New Testament, a person we all can identify with and learn from.

James: His life and letter

This book opens with an excellent portrait of James, who did not believe in Christ when He was on earth, yet who rose to be head of the Jerusalem Church. Then follows a section dealing with the dating of James. The greater part of the book is a clear and useful commentary on the letter, while the concluding section has helpful appendices dealing with (1) unanswered prayer, (2) why James thought it was the last days and (3) why he expected Christ to return soon.

John: His life, death and writings

Peter stands out from amongst the Twelve, being willing to speak and act when others lay silent and still. He was the natural leader and was dominant in the witness to Jews following Christ's resurrection. During those early years Peter was often accompanied by John, who seems to have been his right-hand man, his main support and ally.

This book lays before the reader what the Scriptures have to say about John in chronological order. It also gives an overview of each of his writings and deals with many of the   questions and queries some people have. For example ... Was John the disciple whom Jesus loved? Did he write the Fourth Gospel? Did he die of old age in Ephesus?

Paul: A Missionary of Genius
The life and work of The Apostle to the Gentiles

"One good reason why Christianity was triumphant was that it found in Saul of Tarsus, later St. Paul, a missionary of genius ... Though himself a Jew, Paul took this new and startling religion out of Judaism into the world of the Gentiles," wrote the novelist J B Priestley.

But what do we know about this man Saul, who became Paul? This book covers all his life; from Pharisee to Christian, from Tarsus to Jerusalem, from Antioch to Rome. It also covers his diverse teaching; explaining clearly his two-fold commission to go to the Gentiles as well as Jews, and his later ministry when such distinctions became irrelevant.

Copies of the books on the previous pages can be obtained from

www.obt.org.uk

and from

The Open Bible Trust
Fordland Mount, Upper Basildon,
Reading, RG8 8LU, UK.

They are also available as eBooks from Amazon and Apple
and as paperbacks from Amazon.

Publications of The Open Bible Trust must be in accordance with its evangelical, fundamental and dispensational basis. However, beyond this minimum, writers are free to express whatever beliefs they may have as their own understanding, provided that the aim in so doing is to further the object of The Open Bible Trust. A copy of the doctrinal basis is available on **www.obt.org.uk** or from:

THE OPEN BIBLE TRUST
Fordland Mount, Upper Basildon,
Reading, RG8 8LU, UK